The
U.S. Constitution
For
Christians

The
U.S. Constitution
For
Christians

By
James Garton

Copyright Statement

THE
FIRST PRAYER
IN CONGRESS.

In Thatcher's Military Journal, under date of December, 1777, is found a note containing the identical "First Prayer in Congress," made BY THE REV. J. DUCHE.

O LORD, OUR HEAVENLY FATHER, **high and mighty King of Kings, and Lord of Lords,** who dost from Thy throne behold all the dwellers on earth, and reignest with power supreme and uncontrolled over all the kingdoms, empires and governments; look down in mercy we beseech Thee, on these American States, who have fled to Thee from the rod of the oppressor, and thrown themselves on Thy gracious protection, desiring henceforth to be dependent only on Thee; to Thee they have appealed for the righteousness of their cause; to Thee do they now look up for that countenance and support which Thou alone canst give; take them, therefore, Heavenly Father, under Thy nurturing care; give them wisdom in council and valor in the field; defeat the malicious design of our cruel adversaries; convince them of the unrighteousness of their cause; and if they persist in their sanguinary purpose, O let the voice of Thy own unerring justice, sounding in their hearts, constrain them to drop the weapons of war from their unnerved hands in the day of battle!

Be Thou present, O God of wisdom, and direct the counsels of this honorable assembly; enable them to settle things on the best and surest foundation, that the scene of blood may be speedily closed, that order, harmony and peace may be effectually restored, and truth and justice, religion and piety prevail and flourish among Thy people. Preserve the health of their bodies and vigor of their minds; shower down on them, and the millions they here represent, such temporal blessings as Thou seest expedient for them in this world, and crown them with everlasting glory in the world to come.

All this we ask in the name and through the merits of Jesus Christ, Thy Son, Our Savior.

Amen.

Source: Library of Congress, loc.gov

Preface

For years, I have watched Christians shun the political arena and suffer intimidation and loss of their rights. Our national principals are challenged by organizations and politicians that have an agenda counter to what is right and moral. These groups and political leaders, have no problem outlawing Christian belief as they advocate replacing morality with secular, humanistic, or immoral standards to govern our nation.

We as believers in Christ, must return our nation to its founding principals. These Christian principals and standards, have guided our founders to establish a nation built on equality and liberty. Our liberty, is protected by the U.S. Constitution and was not derived from any government, but our liberty and the promise of equal justice and equal opportunity is endowed to all of us from our creator.

Many have fought and died for your freedom and still to this day, men and women take an oath to support and defend our Constitution and liberty. However, from the founding of our nation, some have yielded to persecution and apathy and departed from the principals they once believed. We must stand firm in our beliefs and never yield to pressure from those who oppose our freedom and Constitution.

My prayer, is that the content of this book, will help you discover your rights and heritage as an American and a follower of **Jesus Christ, Our Lord.**

"Ye are the light of the world. A city that is set on a hill cannot be hid. Neither do men light a candle, and put it under a bushel, but on a candlestick; and it giveth light unto all that are in the house. Let your light so shine before men, that they may see your good works, and glorify your Father which is in heaven." *(Matt. 5:14-16)*

To God Be The Glory!

James Garton

Table of Contents

The First Prayer In Congress............... vi

Preface viii

Preamble of The U.S. Constitution....... 1

Article I 2
Article II 11
Article III 15
Article IV 17
Article V 18
Article VI 19
Article VII 19

Preamble to The Bill of Rights........... 23

Amendment I.....................................24
Amendment II..................................... 24
Amendment III...................................24
Amendment IV................................... 24
Amendment V....................................24
Amendment VI 25
Amendment VII...................................25
Amendment VIII................................... 25
Amendment IX.................................... 25
Amendment X..................................... 26
Amendment XI...................................26
Amendment XII...................................26
Amendment XIII................................... 28
Amendment XIV................................... 28
Amendment XV.................................... 30
Amendment XVI...................................31
Amendment XVII..... 31
Amendment XVIII 32
Amendment XIX...........................32
Amendment XX..................................33
Amendment XXI................................... 34
Amendment XXII.............................35

Amendment XXIII................................ **36**
Amendment XXIV............................... **37**
Amendment XXV................................. **37**
Amendment XXVI............................... **39**
Amendment XXVII.............................. **40**

Quotes From Our Founding Fathers.......**41**

Bible Verses On Government.................. **47**

Quotes From Historic Sermons of Clergy In Support of
Liberty and Moral Government **51**

Declaration of Independence............... **55**

Proposed Seal for The United States.... **65**

The 50 State Constitutions **67**

[**NOTE:** *The following text is a transcription of the Constitution in its original form. Items that are underlined have since been amended or superseded.*]

Source: The National Archives, Archives.gov

𝖂𝖊 𝖙𝖍𝖊 𝕻𝖊𝖔𝖕𝖑𝖊 OF THE UNITED STATES, IN ORDER TO FORM A MORE PERFECT UNION, ESTABLISH JUSTICE, INSURE DOMESTIC TRANQUILITY, PROVIDE FOR THE COMMON DEFENCE, PROMOTE THE GENERAL WELFARE, AND SECURE THE BLESSINGS OF LIBERTY TO OURSELVES AND OUR POSTERITY, DO ORDAIN AND ESTABLISH THIS CONSTITUTION FOR THE UNITED STATES OF AMERICA.

[**NOTE:** *Our founders considered liberty a blessing that we should secure for ourselves and for future generations*]

Article. I.

Section. 1.

All legislative Powers herein granted shall be vested in a Congress of the United States, which shall consist of a Senate and House of Representatives.

Section. 2.

The House of Representatives shall be composed of Members chosen every second Year by the People of the several States, and the Electors in each State shall have the Qualifications requisite for Electors of the most numerous Branch of the State Legislature.

No Person shall be a Representative who shall not have attained to the Age of twenty five Years, and been seven Years a Citizen of the United States, and who shall not, when elected, be an Inhabitant of that State in which he shall be chosen.

Representatives and direct Taxes shall be apportioned among the several States which may be included within this Union, according to their respective Numbers, which shall be determined by adding to the whole Number of free Persons, including those bound to Service for a Term of Years, and excluding Indians not taxed, three fifths of all other Persons. The actual Enumeration shall be made within three Years after the first Meeting of the Congress of the United States, and within every subsequent Term of ten Years, in such Manner as they shall by Law direct.

The Number of Representatives shall not exceed one for every thirty Thousand, but each State shall have at Least one Representative; and until such enumeration shall be made, the State of New Hampshire shall be entitled to chuse three,

Massachusetts eight, Rhode-Island and Providence Plantations one, Connecticut five, New-York six, New Jersey four, Pennsylvania eight, Delaware one, Maryland six, Virginia ten, North Carolina five, South Carolina five, and Georgia three.

When vacancies happen in the Representation from any State, the Executive Authority thereof shall issue Writs of Election to fill such Vacancies.

The House of Representatives shall chuse their Speaker and other Officers; and shall have the sole Power of Impeachment.

Section. 3.

The Senate of the United States shall be composed of two Senators from each State, chosen by the Legislature thereof for six years; and each Senator shall have one Vote.

Immediately after they shall be assembled in Consequence of the first Election, they shall be divided as equally as may be into three Classes. The Seats of the Senators of the first Class shall be vacated at the Expiration of the second Year, of the second Class at the Expiration of the fourth Year, and of the third Class at the Expiration of the sixth Year, so that one third may be chosen every second Year;

and if Vacancies happen by Resignation, or otherwise, during the Recess of the Legislature of any State, the Executive thereof may make temporary Appointments until the next Meeting of the Legislature, which shall then fill such Vacancies.

No Person shall be a Senator who shall not have attained to the Age of thirty Years, and been nine Years a Citizen of the United States, and who shall not, when elected, be an Inhabitant of that State for which he shall be chosen.

The Vice President of the United States shall be President of the Senate, but shall have no Vote, unless they be equally divided.

The Senate shall chuse their other Officers, and also a President pro tempore, in the Absence of the Vice President, or when he shall exercise the Office of President of the United States.

The Senate shall have the sole Power to try all Impeachments. When sitting for that Purpose, they shall be on Oath or Affirmation. When the President of the United States is tried, the Chief Justice shall preside: And no Person shall be convicted without the Concurrence of two thirds of the Members present.

Judgment in Cases of impeachment shall not extend further than to removal from Office, and disqualification to hold and enjoy any Office of honor, Trust or Profit under the United States: but the Party convictcd shall nevertheless be liable and subject to Indictment, Trial, Judgment and Punishment, according to Law.

Section. 4.

The Times, Places and Manner of holding Elections for Senators and Representatives, shall be prescribed in each State by the Legislature thereof; but the Congress may at any time by Law make or alter such Regulations, except as to the Places of chusing Senators.

The Congress shall assemble at least once in every Year, and such Meeting shall <u>be on the first Monday in December,</u> unless they shall by Law appoint a different Day.

Section. 5.

Each House shall be the Judge of the Elections, Returns and Qualifications of its own Members, and a Majority of each shall constitute a Quorum to do Business; but a smaller Number may adjourn from day to day, and may be authorized to compel the Attendance of absent Members, in such Manner, and under such Penalties as each House may provide.

Each House may determine the Rules of its Proceedings, punish its Members for disorderly Behaviour, and, with the Concurrence of two thirds, expel a Member.

Each House shall keep a Journal of its Proceedings, and from time to time publish the same, excepting such Parts as may in their Judgment require Secrecy; and the Yeas and Nays of the Members of either House on any question shall, at the Desire of one fifth of those Present, be entered on the Journal.

Neither House, during the Session of Congress, shall, without the Consent of the other, adjourn for more than three days, nor to any other Place than that in which the two Houses shall be sitting.

Section. 6.

The Senators and Representatives shall receive a Compensation for their Services, to be ascertained by Law, and paid out of the Treasury of the United States. They shall in all Cases,

except Treason, Felony and Breach of the Peace, be privileged from Arrest during their Attendance at the Session of their respective Houses, and in going to and returning from the same; and for any Speech or Debate in either House, they shall not be questioned in any other Place.

No Senator or Representative shall, during the Time for which he was elected, be appointed to any civil Office under the Authority of the United States, which shall have been created, or the Emoluments whereof shall have been encreased during such time; and no Person holding any Office under the United States, shall be a Member of either House during his Continuance in Office.

Section. 7.

All Bills for raising Revenue shall originate in the House of Representatives; but the Senate may propose or concur with Amendments as on other Bills.

Every Bill which shall have passed the House of Representatives and the Senate, shall, before it become a Law, be presented to the President of the United States: If he approve he shall sign it, but if not he shall return it, with his Objections to that House in which it shall have originated, who shall enter the Objections at large on their Journal, and proceed to reconsider it. If after such Reconsideration two thirds of that House shall agree to pass the Bill, it shall be sent, together with the Objections, to the other House, by which it shall likewise be reconsidered, and if approved by two thirds of that House, it shall become a Law. But in all such Cases the Votes of both Houses shall be determined by yeas and Nays, and the Names of the Persons voting for and against the Bill shall be entered on the Journal of each House respectively. If any Bill shall not be returned by the President within ten Days (Sundays excepted) after it shall have been presented to him, the Same shall be a Law, in like Manner as if he had signed it, unless the Congress by their Adjournment prevent its Return, in which Case it shall not be a Law.

Every Order, Resolution, or Vote to which the Concurrence of the Senate and House of Representatives may be necessary (except on a question of Adjournment) shall be presented to the President of the United States; and before the Same shall take Effect, shall be approved by him, or being disapproved by him, shall be repassed by two thirds of the Senate and House of Representatives, according to the Rules and Limitations prescribed in the Case of a Bill.

Section. 8.

The Congress shall have Power To lay and collect Taxes, Duties, Imposts and Excises, to pay the Debts and provide for the common Defence and general Welfare of the United States; but all Duties, Imposts and Excises shall be uniform throughout the United States;

To borrow Money on the credit of the United States;

To regulate Commerce with foreign Nations, and among the several States, and with the Indian Tribes;

To establish an uniform Rule of Naturalization, and uniform

Laws on the subject of Bankruptcies throughout the United States;

To coin Money, regulate the Value thereof, and of foreign Coin, and fix the Standard of Weights and Measures;

To provide for the Punishment of counterfeiting the Securities and current Coin of the United States;

To establish Post Offices and post Roads;

To promote the Progress of Science and useful Arts, by securing for limited Times to Authors and Inventors the exclusive Right to their respective Writings and Discoveries;

To constitute Tribunals inferior to the supreme Court;

To define and punish Piracies and Felonies committed on the

high Seas, and Offences against

the Law of Nations;

To declare War, grant Letters of Marque and Reprisal, and make Rules concerning Captures on Land and Water;

To raise and support Armies, but no Appropriation of Money to that Use shall be for a longer Term than two Years;

To provide and maintain a Navy;

To make Rules for the Government and Regulation of the land and naval Forces;

To provide for calling forth the Militia to execute the Laws of the Union, suppress Insurrections and repel

Invasions;

To provide for organizing, arming, and disciplining, the Militia, and for governing such Part of them as may be employed in the Service of the United States, reserving to the States respectively, the Appointment of the Officers, and the Authority of

training the Militia according to the discipline prescribed by Congress;

To exercise exclusive Legislation in all Cases whatsoever, over such District (not exceeding ten Miles square) as may, by Cession of particular States, and the Acceptance of Congress, become the Seat of the Government of the United States, and to exercise like Authority over all Places purchased by the Consent of the Legislature of the State in which the Same shall be, for the Erection of Forts, Magazines, Arsenals, dock-Yards, and other needful Buildings;--And To make all Laws which shall be necessary and proper for carrying into Execution the foregoing Powers, and all other Powers vested by this Constitution in the Government of the United States, or in any Department or Officer thereof.

Section. 9.

The Migration or Importation of such Persons as any of the States now existing shall think proper to admit, shall not be prohibited by the Congress prior to the Year one thousand eight hundred and eight, but a Tax or duty may be imposed on such Importation, not exceeding ten dollars for each Person.

The Privilege of the Writ of Habeas Corpus shall not be suspended, unless when in Cases of Rebellion or Invasion the public Safety may require it.

No Bill of Attainder or ex post facto Law shall be passed.

No Capitation, or other direct, Tax shall be laid, <u>unless in Proportion to the Census or enumeration herein before directed to be taken.</u>

No Tax or Duty shall be laid on Articles exported from any State.

No Preference shall be given by any Regulation of Commerce or Revenue to the Ports of one State over those of another; nor shall Vessels bound to, or from, one State, be obliged to enter, clear, or pay Duties in another.

No Money shall be drawn from the Treasury, but in Consequence of Appropriations made by Law; and a regular Statement and Account of the Receipts and Expenditures of all public Money shall be published from time to time.

No Title of Nobility shall be granted by the United States: And no Person holding any Office of Profit or Trust under them, shall, without the Consent of the Congress, accept of any present, Emolument, Office, or Title, of any kind whatever, from any King, Prince, or foreign State.

Section. 10.

No State shall enter into any Treaty, Alliance, or Confederation; grant Letters of Marque and Reprisal; coin Money; emit Bills of Credit; make any Thing but gold and silver Coin a Tender in Payment of Debts; pass any Bill of Attainder, ex post facto Law, or Law impairing the Obligation of Contracts, or grant any Title of Nobility.

No State shall, without the Consent of the Congress, lay any Imposts or Duties on Imports or Exports, except what may be absolutely necessary for executing it's inspection Laws: and the net Produce of all Duties and Imposts, laid by any State on Imports or Exports, shall be for the Use of the Treasury of the United States; and all such Laws shall be subject to the Revision and Controul of the Congress.

No State shall, without the Consent of Congress, lay any Duty of Tonnage, keep Troops, or Ships of War in time of Peace, enter into any Agreement or Compact with another State, or with a foreign Power, or engage in War, unless actually invaded, or in such imminent danger as will not admit of delay.

Article. II.

Section. 1.

The executive Power shall be vested in a President of the United States of America. He shall hold his Office during the Term of four Years, and, together with the Vice President, chosen for the same Term, be elected, as follows:

Each State shall appoint, in such Manner as the Legislature thereof may direct, a Number of Electors, equal to the whole Number of Senators and Representatives to which the State may be entitled in the Congress: but no Senator or Representative, or Person holding an Office of Trust or Profit under the United States, shall be appointed an Elector.

The Electors shall meet in their respective States, and vote by Ballot for two Persons, of whom one at least shall not be an Inhabitant of the same State with themselves. And they shall make a List of all the Persons voted for, and of the Number of Votes for each; which List they shall sign and certify, and transmit sealed to the Seat of the Government of the United States, directed to the President of the Senate. The President of the Senate shall, in the Presence of the Senate and House of Representatives, open all the Certificates, and the Votes shall then be counted. The Person having the greatest Number of Votes shall be the President, if such Number be a Majority of the whole Number of Electors appointed; and if there be more than one who have such Majority, and have an equal Number of Votes, then the House of Representatives shall immediately chuse by Ballot one of them for President; and if no Person have a Majority, then from the five highest on the List the said House shall in like Manner chuse the President. But in chusing the President, the Votes shall be taken by States, the Representation from each State having one Vote; A quorum for this purpose shall consist of a Member or Members from two thirds of the States, and a Majority of all the States shall be necessary to a Choice. In every Case, after the Choice of the President, the Person having the greatest Number of Votes of the Electors shall be the Vice President. But if there should remain two or more who have equal Votes, the Senate shall chuse from them by Ballot the Vice President.

The Congress may determine the Time of chusing the Electors, and the Day on which they shall give their Votes; which Day shall be the same throughout the United States.

No Person except a natural born Citizen, or a Citizen of the United States, at the time of the Adoption of this Constitution, shall be eligible to the Office of President; neither shall any Person be eligible to that Office who shall not have attained to the Age of thirty five Years, and been fourteen Years a Resident within the United States.

In Case of the Removal of the President from Office, or of his Death, Resignation, or Inability to discharge the Powers and Duties of the said Office, the Same shall devolve on the Vice President, and the Congress may by Law provide for the Case of Removal, Death, Resignation or Inability, both of the President and Vice President, declaring what Officer shall then act as President, and such Officer shall act accordingly, until the Disability be removed, or a President shall be elected.

The President shall, at stated Times, receive for his Services, a Compensation, which shall neither be increased nor diminished during the Period for which he shall have been elected, and he shall not receive within that Period any other Emolument from the United States, or any of them.

Before he enter on the Execution of his Office, he shall take the following Oath or Affirmation:--"I do solemnly swear (or affirm) that I will faithfully execute the Office of President of the United States, and will to the best of my Ability, preserve, protect and defend the Constitution of the United States."

Section. 2.

The President shall be Commander in Chief of the Army and Navy of the United States, and of the Militia of the several States, when called into the actual Service of the United States; he may require the Opinion, in writing, of the principal Officer in each of the executive Departments, upon any Subject relating to the Duties of their respective Offices, and he shall have Power to grant Reprieves and Pardons for Offences against the United States, except in Cases of

Impeachment.

He shall have Power, by and with the Advice and Consent of the Senate, to make Treaties, provided two thirds of the Senators present concur; and he shall nominate, and by and with the Advice and Consent of the Senate, shall appoint Ambassadors, other public Ministers and Consuls, Judges of the supreme Court, and all other Officers of the United States, whose Appointments are not herein otherwise provided for, and which shall be established by Law: but the Congress may by Law vest the Appointment of such inferior Officers, as they think proper, in the President alone, in the Courts of Law, or in the Heads of Departments.

The President shall have Power to fill up all Vacancies that may happen during the Recess of the Senate, by granting Commissions which shall expire at the End of their next Session.

Section. 3.

He shall from time to time give to the Congress Information of the State of the Union, and recommend to their Consideration such Measures as he shall judge necessary and expedient; he may, on extraordinary Occasions, convene both Houses, or either of them, and in Case of Disagreement between them, with Respect to the Time of Adjournment, he may adjourn them to such Time as he shall think proper; he shall receive Ambassadors and other public Ministers; he shall take Care that the Laws be faithfully executed, and shall Commission all the Officers of the United States.

Section. 4.

The President, Vice President and all civil Officers of the United States, shall be removed from Office on Impeachment for, and Conviction of, Treason, Bribery, or other high Crimes and Misdemeanors.

Article III.

Section. 1.

The judicial Power of the United States shall be vested in one supreme Court, and in such inferior Courts as the Congress may from time to time ordain and establish. The Judges, both of the supreme and inferior Courts, shall hold their Offices during good Behaviour, and shall, at stated Times, receive for their Services a Compensation, which shall not be diminished during their Continuance in Office.

Section. 2.

The judicial Power shall extend to all Cases, in Law and Equity, arising under this Constitution, the Laws of the United States, and Treaties made, or which shall be made, under their Authority;--to all Cases affecting Ambassadors, other public Ministers and Consuls;--to all Cases of admiralty and maritime Jurisdiction;--to Controversies to which the United States shall be a Party;--to Controversies between two or more States;-- between a State and Citizens of another State,-- between Citizens of different States,--between Citizens of the same State claiming Lands under Grants of different States, and between a State, or the Citizens thereof, and foreign States, Citizens or Subjects.

In all Cases affecting Ambassadors, other public Ministers and Consuls, and those in which a State shall be Party, the supreme Court shall have original Jurisdiction. In all the other Cases before mentioned, the supreme Court shall have appellate Jurisdiction, both as to Law and Fact, with such Exceptions, and under such Regulations as the Congress shall make.

The Trial of all Crimes, except in Cases of Impeachment, shall be by Jury; and such Trial shall be held in the State where the said Crimes shall have been committed; but when not committed within any State, the Trial shall be at such Place or Places as the Congress may by Law have directed.

Section. 3.

Treason against the United States, shall consist only in levying War against them, or in adhering to their Enemies, giving them Aid and Comfort. No Person shall be convicted of Treason unless on the Testimony of two Witnesses to the same overt Act, or on Confession in open Court.

The Congress shall have Power to declare the Punishment of Treason, but no Attainder of Treason shall work Corruption of Blood, or Forfeiture except during the Life of the Person attainted.

Article. IV.

Section. 1.

Full Faith and Credit shall be given in each State to the public Acts, Records, and judicial Proceedings of every other State. And the Congress may by general Laws prescribe the Manner in which such Acts, Records and Proceedings shall be proved, and the Effect thereof.

Section. 2.

The Citizens of each State shall be entitled to all Privileges and Immunities of Citizens in the several States.

A Person charged in any State with Treason, Felony, or other Crime, who shall flee from Justice, and be found in another State, shall on Demand of the executive Authority of the State from which he fled, be delivered up, to be removed to the State having Jurisdiction of the Crime.

No Person held to Service or Labour in one State, under the Laws thereof, escaping into another, shall, in Consequence of any Law or Regulation therein, be discharged from such Service or Labour, but shall be delivered up on Claim of the Party to whom such Service or Labour may be due.

Section. 3.

New States may be admitted by the Congress into this Union; but no new State shall be formed or erected within the Jurisdiction of any other State; nor any State be formed by the Junction of two or more States, or Parts of States, without the Consent of the Legislatures of the States concerned as well as of the Congress.

The Congress shall have Power to dispose of and make all needful Rules and Regulations respecting the Territory or other Property belonging to the United States; and nothing in this Constitution shall be so construed as to Prejudice any Claims of the United States, or of any particular State.

Section. 4.

The United States shall guarantee to every State in this Union a Republican Form of Government, and shall protect each of them against Invasion; and on Application of the Legislature, or of the Executive (when the Legislature cannot be convened), against domestic Violence.

Article. V.

The Congress, whenever two thirds of both Houses shall deem it necessary, shall propose Amendments to this Constitution, or, on the Application of the Legislatures of two thirds of the several States, shall call a Convention for proposing Amendments, which, in either Case, shall be valid to all Intents and Purposes, as Part of this Constitution, when ratified by the Legislatures of three fourths of the several States, or by Conventions in three fourths thereof, as the one or the other Mode of Ratification may be proposed by the Congress; Provided that no Amendment which may be made prior to the Year One thousand eight hundred and eight shall in any Manner affect the first and fourth Clauses in the Ninth Section of the first Article; and that no State, without its Consent, shall be deprived of its equal Suffrage in the Senate.

Article. VI.

All Debts contracted and Engagements entered into, before the Adoption of this Constitution, shall be as valid against the United States under this Constitution, as under the Confederation.

This Constitution, and the Laws of the United States which shall be made in Pursuance thereof; and all Treaties made, or which shall be made, under the Authority of the United States, shall be the supreme Law of the Land; and the Judges in every State shall be bound thereby, any Thing in the Constitution or Laws of any State to the Contrary notwithstanding.

The Senators and Representatives before mentioned, and the Members of

the several State Legislatures, and all executive and judicial Officers, both of the United States and of the several States, shall be bound by Oath or Affirmation, to support this Constitution; but no religious Test shall ever be required as a Qualification to any Office or public Trust under the United States.

Article. VII.

The Ratification of the Conventions of nine States, shall be sufficient for the Establishment of this Constitution between the States so ratifying the Same.

The Word, "the," being interlined between the seventh and eighth Lines of the first Page, the Word "Thirty" being partly written on an Erazure in

the fifteenth Line of the first Page, The Words "is tried" being interlined between the thirty second and thirty third Lines of the first Page and the Word "the" being interlined between the forty third and forty fourth Lines of the second Page.

Attest **William Jackson Secretary**

done in Convention by the Unanimous Consent of the States present the Seventeenth Day of September in the Year of our Lord one thousand seven hundred and Eighty seven and of the Independance of the United States of America the Twelfth In witness whereof We have hereunto subscribed our Names,

G°. Washington
Presidt and deputy from Virginia

Delaware
Geo: Read
Gunning Bedford jun
John Dickinson
Richard Bassett
Jaco: Broom

Maryland
James McHenry
Dan of St Thos. Jenifer
Danl. Carroll

Virginia
John Blair
James Madison Jr.

North Carolina
Wm. Blount
Richd. Dobbs Spaight
Hu Williamson

South Carolina
J. Rutledge
Charles Cotesworth Pinckney
Charles Pinckney
Pierce Butler

Georgia
William Few
Abr Baldwin

New Hampshire
John Langdon
Nicholas Gilman

Massachusetts
Nathaniel Gorham
Rufus King

Connecticut
Wm. Saml. Johnson
Roger Sherman

New York
Alexander Hamilton

New Jersey
Wil: Livingston
David Brearley
Wm. Paterson
Jona: Dayton

Pennsylvania
B Franklin
Thomas Mifflin
Robt. Morris
Geo. Clymer
Thos. FitzSimons
Jared Ingersoll
James Wilson
Gouv Morris

The Preamble to The Bill of Rights

Congress of the United States
begun and held at the City of New-York, on Wednesday the fourth of March, one thousand seven hundred and eighty nine.

THE Conventions of a number of the States, having at the time of their adopting the Constitution, expressed a desire, in order to prevent misconstruction or abuse of its powers, that further declaratory and restrictive clauses should be added: And as extending the ground of public confidence in the Government, will best ensure the beneficent ends of its institution.

RESOLVED by the Senate and House of Representatives of the United States of America, in Congress assembled, two thirds of both Houses concurring, that the following Articles be proposed to the Legislatures of the several States, as amendments to the Constitution of the United States, all, or any of which Articles, when ratified by three fourths of the said Legislatures, to be valid to all intents and purposes, as part of the said Constitution; viz.

ARTICLES in addition to, and Amendment of the Constitution of the United States of America, proposed by Congress, and ratified by the Legislatures of the several States, pursuant to the fifth Article of the original Constitution.

[**NOTE**: *The following text is a transcription of the first ten amendments to the Constitution in their original form. These amendments were ratified December 15, 1791, and form what is known as the "Bill of Rights."*]

Amendment I

Congress shall make no law respecting an establishment of religion, or prohibiting the free exercise thereof; or abridging the freedom of speech, or of the press; or the right of the people peaceably to assemble, and to petition the Government for a redress of grievances.

Amendment II

A well regulated Militia, being necessary to the security of a free State, the right of the people to keep and bear Arms, shall not be infringed.

Amendment III

No Soldier shall, in time of peace be quartered in any house, without the consent of the Owner, nor in time of war, but in a manner to be prescribed by law.

Amendment IV

The right of the people to be secure in their persons, houses, papers, and effects, against unreasonable searches and seizures, shall not be violated, and no Warrants shall issue, but upon probable cause, supported by Oath or affirmation, and particularly describing the place to be searched, and the persons or things to be seized.

Amendment V

No person shall be held to answer for a capital, or otherwise infamous crime, unless on a presentment or indictment of a Grand Jury, except in cases arising in the land or naval forces, or in the Militia, when in actual service in time of War or public danger; nor shall any person be subject for the same offence to be twice put in jeopardy of life or limb; nor shall be compelled in any criminal case to be a witness against himself, nor be deprived of life, liberty, or property, without due process of law; nor shall private property be taken for public use, without just compensation.

Amendment VI

In all criminal prosecutions, the accused shall enjoy the right to a speedy and public trial, by an impartial jury of the State and district wherein the crime shall have been committed, which district shall have been previously ascertained by law, and to be informed of the nature and cause of the accusation; to be confronted with the witnesses against him; to have compulsory process for obtaining witnesses in his favor, and to have the Assistance of Counsel for his defence.

Amendment VII

In Suits at common law, where the value in controversy shall exceed twenty dollars, the right of trial by jury shall be preserved, and no fact tried by a jury, shall be otherwise re-examined in any Court of the United States, than according to the rules of the common law.

Amendment VIII

Excessive bail shall not be required, nor excessive fines imposed, nor cruel and unusual punishments inflicted.

Amendment IX

The enumeration in the Constitution, of certain rights, shall not be construed to deny or disparage others retained by the people.

Amendment X

The powers not delegated to the United States by the Constitution, nor prohibited by it to the States, are reserved to the States respectively, or to the people.

AMENDMENT XI

Passed by Congress March 4, 1794. Ratified February 7, 1795.

[**NOTE:** *Article III, section 2, of the Constitution was modified by amendment 11.*]

The Judicial power of the United States shall not be construed to extend to any suit in law or equity, commenced or prosecuted against one of the United States by Citizens of another State, or by Citizens or Subjects of any Foreign State.

AMENDMENT XII

Passed by Congress December 9, 1803. Ratified June 15, 1804.

[**NOTE:** *A portion of Article II, section 1 of the Constitution was superseded by the 12th amendment.*]

The Electors shall meet in their respective states and vote by ballot for President and Vice-President, one of whom, at least, shall not be an inhabitant of the same state with themselves; they shall name in their ballots the person voted for as President, and in distinct ballots the person voted for as Vice-President, and they shall make distinct lists of all persons voted for as President, and of all persons voted for as Vice-President, and of the number of votes for each, which lists they shall sign and certify, and transmit sealed to the seat of the government of the United States, directed to the President of the Senate; -- the President of the Senate shall, in the presence of the Senate and House of Representatives, open all the certificates and the votes shall then be counted; -- The person having the greatest number of votes for President, shall be the President, if such number be a majority of the whole number of Electors appointed; and if no person have such majority, then from the persons having the highest numbers not exceeding three on the list of those voted for as President, the House of Representatives shall choose immediately, by ballot, the President. But in choosing the President, the votes shall be taken by states, the representation from each state having one vote; a quorum for this purpose shall consist of a member or members from two-thirds of the states, and a majority of all the states shall be necessary to a choice. [And if the House of Representatives shall not choose a President whenever the right of choice shall devolve upon them, before the fourth day of March next following, then the Vice-President shall act as President, as in case of the death or other constitutional disability of the President. --]* The person having the greatest number of votes as Vice-President, shall be the Vice-President, if such number be a majority of the whole number of Electors appointed, and if no person have a majority, then from the two highest numbers on the list, the Senate shall choose the Vice-President; a quorum for the purpose shall consist of two-thirds of the whole number of Senators, and a majority of the whole number shall be necessary to a choice. But no person constitutionally ineligible to the office of President shall be eligible to that of Vice-President of the United States.

*Superseded by section 3 of the 20th amendment.

AMENDMENT XIII

Passed by Congress January 31, 1865. Ratified December 6, 1865.

[NOTE: *A portion of Article IV, section 2, of the Constitution was superseded by the 13th amendment.***]**

Section 1.

Neither slavery nor involuntary servitude, except as a punishment for crime whereof the party shall have been duly convicted, shall exist within the United States, or any place subject to their jurisdiction.

Section 2.

Congress shall have power to enforce this article by appropriate legislation.

AMENDMENT XIV

Passed by Congress June 13, 1866. Ratified July 9, 1868.

[NOTE: *Article I, section 2, of the Constitution was modified by section 2 of the 14th amendment.***]**

Section 1.

All persons born or naturalized in the United States, and subject to the jurisdiction thereof, are citizens of the United States and of the State wherein they reside. No State shall make or enforce any law which shall abridge the privileges or immunities of citizens of the United States; nor shall any State deprive any person of life, liberty, or property, without due process of law; nor deny to any person within its jurisdiction the equal protection of the laws.

Section 2.

Representatives shall be apportioned among the several States according to their respective numbers, counting the whole number of persons in each State, excluding Indians not taxed. But when the right to vote at any election for the choice of electors for President and Vice-President of the United States, Representatives in Congress, the Executive and Judicial officers of a State, or the members of the Legislature thereof, is denied to any of the male inhabitants of such State, being twenty-one years of age,* and citizens of the United States, or in any way abridged, except for participation in rebellion, or other crime, the basis of representation therein shall be reduced in the proportion which the number of such male citizens shall bear to the whole number of male citizens twenty-one years of age in such State.

Section 3.

No person shall be a Senator or Representative in Congress, or elector of President and Vice-President, or hold any office, civil or military, under the United States, or under any State, who, having previously taken an oath, as a member of Congress, or as an officer of the United States, or as a member of any State legislature, or as an executive or judicial officer of any State, to support the Constitution of the United States, shall have engaged in insurrection or rebellion against the same, or given aid or comfort to the enemies thereof. But Congress may by a vote of two-thirds of each House, remove such disability.

Section 4.

The validity of the public debt of the United States, authorized by law, including debts incurred for payment of pensions and bounties for services in suppressing insurrection or rebellion, shall not be questioned. But neither the United States nor any State shall assume or pay any debt or obligation incurred in aid of insurrection or rebellion against the United States, or any claim for the loss or emancipation of any slave; but all such debts, obligations and claims shall be held illegal and void.

Section 5.

The Congress shall have the power to enforce, by appropriate legislation, the provisions of this article.

*Changed by section 1 of the 26th amendment.

AMENDMENT XV

Passed by Congress February 26, 1869. Ratified February 3, 1870.

Section 1.

The right of citizens of the United States to vote shall not be denied or abridged by the United States or by any State on account of race, color, or previous condition of servitude--

Section 2.

The Congress shall have the power to enforce this article by appropriate legislation.

AMENDMENT XVI

Passed by Congress July 2, 1909. Ratified February 3, 1913.

[**NOTE:** *Article I, section 9, of the Constitution was modified by amendment 16.*]

The Congress shall have power to lay and collect taxes on incomes, from whatever source derived, without apportionment among the several States, and without regard to any census or enumeration.

AMENDMENT XVII

Passed by Congress May 13, 1912. Ratified April 8, 1913.

[**NOTE:** *Article I, section 3, of the Constitution was modified by the 17th amendment.*]

The Senate of the United States shall be composed of two Senators from each State, elected by the people thereof, for six years; and each Senator shall have one vote. The electors in each State shall have the qualifications requisite for electors of the most numerous branch of the State legislatures.

When vacancies happen in the representation of any State in the Senate, the executive authority of such State shall issue writs of election to fill such vacancies:

Provided, That the legislature of any State may empower the executive thereof to make temporary appointments until the people fill the vacancies by election as the legislature may direct.

This amendment shall not be so construed as to affect the election or term of any Senator chosen before it becomes valid as part of the Constitution.

AMENDMENT XVIII

Passed by Congress December 18, 1917. Ratified January 16, 1919. Repealed by amendment 21.

Section 1.

After one year from the ratification of this article the manufacture, sale, or transportation of intoxicating liquors within, the importation thereof into, or the exportation thereof from the United States and all territory subject to the jurisdiction thereof for beverage purposes is hereby prohibited.

Section 2.

The Congress and the several States shall have concurrent power to enforce this article by appropriate legislation.

Section 3.

This article shall be inoperative unless it shall have been ratified as an amendment to the Constitution by the legislatures of the several States, as provided in the Constitution, within seven years from the date of the submission hereof to the States by the Congress.

AMENDMENT XIX

Passed by Congress June 4, 1919. Ratified August 18, 1920.

The right of citizens of the United States to vote shall not be denied or abridged by the United States or by any State on account of sex.

Congress shall have power to enforce this article by appropriate legislation.

AMENDMENT XX

Passed by Congress March 2, 1932. Ratified January 23, 1933.

[NOTE: *Article I, section 4, of the Constitution was modified by section 2 of this amendment. In addition, a portion of the 12th amendment was superseded by section 3.*]

Section 1.

The terms of the President and the Vice President shall end at noon on the 20th day of January, and the terms of Senators and Representatives at noon on the 3d day of January, of the years in which such terms would have ended if this article had not been ratified; and the terms of their successors shall then begin.

Section 2.

The Congress shall assemble at least once in every year, and such meeting shall begin at noon on the 3d day of January, unless they shall by law appoint a different day.

Section 3.

If, at the time fixed for the beginning of the term of the President, the President elect shall have died, the Vice President elect shall become President. If a President shall not have been chosen before the time fixed for the beginning of his term, or if the President elect shall have failed to qualify, then the Vice President elect shall act as President until a President shall have qualified; and the Congress may by law provide for the case wherein neither a President elect nor a Vice President shall have qualified, declaring who shall then act as President, or the manner in which one who is to act shall be selected, and such person shall act accordingly until a President or Vice President shall have qualified.

Section 4.

The Congress may by law provide for the case of the death of any of the persons from whom the House of Representatives may choose a President whenever the right of choice shall have devolved upon them, and for the case of the death of any of the persons from whom the Senate may choose a Vice President whenever the right of choice shall have devolved upon them.

Section 5.

Sections 1 and 2 shall take effect on the 15th day of October following the ratification of this article.

Section 6.

This article shall be inoperative unless it shall have been ratified as an amendment to the Constitution by the legislatures of three-fourths of the several States within seven years from the date of its submission.

AMENDMENT XXI

Passed by Congress February 20, 1933. Ratified December 5, 1933.

Section 1.

The eighteenth article of amendment to the Constitution of the United States is hereby repealed.

Section 2.

The transportation or importation into any State, Territory, or Possession of the United States for delivery or use therein of intoxicating liquors, in violation of the laws thereof, is hereby prohibited.

Section 3.

This article shall be inoperative unless it shall have been ratified as an amendment to the Constitution by conventions in the several States, as provided in the Constitution, within seven years from the date of the submission hereof to the States by the Congress.

AMENDMENT XXII

Passed by Congress March 21, 1947. Ratified February 27, 1951.

Section 1.

No person shall be elected to the office of the President more than twice, and no person who has held the office of President, or acted as President, for more than two years of a term to which some other person was elected President shall be elected to the office of President more than once. But this Article shall not apply to any person holding the office of President when this Article was proposed by Congress, and shall not prevent any person who may be holding the office of President, or acting as President, during the term within which this Article becomes operative from holding the office of President or acting as President during the remainder of such term.

Section 2.

This article shall be inoperative unless it shall have been ratified as an amendment to the Constitution by the legislatures of three-fourths of the several States within seven years from the date of its submission to the States by the Congress.

AMENDMENT XXIII

Passed by Congress June 16, 1960. Ratified March 29, 1961.

Section 1.

The District constituting the seat of Government of the United States shall appoint in such manner as Congress may direct:

A number of electors of President and Vice President equal to the whole number of Senators and Representatives in Congress to which the District would be entitled if it were a State, but in no event more than the least populous State; they shall be in addition to those appointed by the States, but they shall be considered, for the purposes of the election of President and Vice President, to be electors appointed by a State; and they shall meet in the District and perform such duties as provided by the twelfth article of amendment.

Section 2.

The Congress shall have power to enforce this article by appropriate legislation.

AMENDMENT XXIV

Passed by Congress August 27, 1962. Ratified January 23, 1964.

Section 1.

The right of citizens of the United States to vote in any primary or other election for President or Vice President, for electors for President or Vice President, or for Senator or Representative in Congress, shall not be denied or abridged by the United States or any State by reason of failure to pay poll tax or other tax.

Section 2.

The Congress shall have power to enforce this article by appropriate legislation.

AMENDMENT XXV

Passed by Congress July 6, 1965. Ratified February 10, 1967.
Note: Article II, section 1, of the Constitution was affected by the 25th amendment.

Section 1.

In case of the removal of the President from office or of his death or resignation, the Vice President shall become President.

Section 2.

Whenever there is a vacancy in the office of the Vice President, the President shall nominate a Vice President who shall take office upon confirmation by a majority vote of both Houses of Congress.

Section 3.

Whenever the President transmits to the President pro tempore of the Senate and the Speaker of the House of Representatives his written declaration that he is unable to discharge the powers and duties of his office, and until he transmits to them a written declaration to the contrary, such powers and duties shall be discharged by the Vice President as Acting President.

Section 4.

Whenever the Vice President and a majority of either the principal officers of the executive departments or of such other body as Congress may by law provide, transmit to the President pro tempore of the Senate and the Speaker of the House of Representatives their written declaration that the President is unable to discharge the powers and duties of his office, the Vice President shall immediately assume the powers and duties of the office as Acting President.

Thereafter, when the President transmits to the President pro tempore of the Senate and the Speaker of the House of Representatives his written declaration that no inability exists, he shall resume the powers and duties of his office unless the Vice President and a majority of either the principal officers of the executive department or of such other body as Congress may by law provide, transmit within four days to the President pro tempore of the Senate and the Speaker of the House of Representatives their written declaration that the President is unable to discharge the powers and duties of his office.

Thereupon Congress shall decide the issue, assembling within forty-eight hours for that purpose if not in session. If the Congress, within twenty-one days after receipt of the latter written declaration, or, if Congress is not in session, within twenty-one days after Congress is required to assemble, determines by two-thirds vote of both Houses that the President is unable to discharge the powers and duties of his office, the Vice President shall continue to discharge the same as Acting President; otherwise, the President shall resume the powers and duties of his office.

AMENDMENT XXVI

Passed by Congress March 23, 1971. Ratified July 1, 1971.

[NOTE: *Amendment 14, section 2, of the Constitution was modified by section 1 of the 26th amendment.***]**

Section 1.

The right of citizens of the United States, who are eighteen years of age or older, to vote shall not be denied or abridged by the United States or by any State on account of age.

Section 2.

The Congress shall have power to enforce this article by appropriate legislation.

AMENDMENT XXVII

Originally proposed Sept. 25, 1789. Ratified May 7, 1992.

No law, varying the compensation for the services of the Senators and Representatives, shall take effect, until an election of representatives shall have intervened.

Quotes From Our Founding Fathers

George Washington

1st U.S. President

"While we are zealously performing the duties of good citizens and soldiers, we certainly ought not to be inattentive to the higher duties of religion. To the distinguished character of Patriot, it should be our highest glory to add the more distinguished character of Christian."

– The Writings of Washington, pp. 342-343.

"[T]he [federal] government . . . can never be in danger of degenerating into a monarchy, and oligarchy, an aristocracy, or any other despotic or oppressive form so long as there shall remain any virtue in the body of the people."

– George Washington, The Writings of George Washington, John C. Fitzpatrick, editor (Washington: U. S. Government Printing Office, 1939), Vol. XXIX, p. 410. In a letter to Marquis De Lafayette, February 7, 1788.

John Adams

2nd U.S. President and Signer of the Declaration of Independence

"Suppose a nation in some distant Region should take the Bible for their only law Book, and every member should regulate his conduct by the precepts there exhibited! Every member would be obliged in conscience, to temperance, frugality, and industry; to justice, kindness, and charity towards his fellow men; and to piety, love, and reverence toward Almighty God ... What a Eutopia, what a Paradise would this region be."

 – *Diary and Autobiography of John Adams, Vol. III, p. 9.*

"We have no government armed with power capable of contending with human passions unbridled by morality and religion. . . . Our constitution was made only for a moral and religious people. It is wholly inadequate to the government of any other."

– *John Adams, The Works of John Adams, Second President of the United States, Charles Francis Adams, editor (Boston: Little, Brown, and Co. 1854), Vol. IX, p. 229, October 11, 1798.)*

Thomas Jefferson

3rd U.S. President, Drafter and Signer of the Declaration of Independence

"God who gave us life gave us liberty. And can the liberties of a nation be thought secure when we have removed their only firm basis, a conviction in the minds of the people that these liberties are of the Gift of God? That they are not to be violated but with His wrath? Indeed, I tremble for my country when I reflect that God is just; that His justice cannot sleep forever; That a revolution of the wheel of fortune, a change of situation, is among possible events; that it may become probable by Supernatural influence! The Almighty has no attribute which can take side with us in that event."

— Notes on the State of Virginia, Query XVIII, p. 237.

John Hancock

1st Signer of the Declaration of Independence

"Resistance to tyranny becomes the Christian and social duty of each individual. ... Continue steadfast and, with a proper sense of your dependence on God, nobly defend those rights which heaven gave, and no man ought to take from us."

— History of the United States of America, Vol. II, p. 229.

James Monroe

5th U.S. President

"When we view the blessings with which our country has been favored, those which we now enjoy, and the means which we possess of handing them down unimpaired to our latest posterity, our attention is irresistibly drawn to the source from whence they flow. Let us then, unite in offering our most grateful acknowledgments for these blessings to the Divine Author of All Good."

– Monroe made this statement in his 2nd Annual Message to Congress, November 16, 1818.

Benjamin Rush

Signer of the Declaration of Independence and Ratifier of the U.S. Constitution

"The gospel of Jesus Christ prescribes the wisest rules for just conduct in every situation of life. Happy they who are enabled to obey them in all situations!"

– The Autobiography of Benjamin Rush, pp. 165-166.

"The only foundation for a useful education in a republic is to be laid in religion. Without this there can be no virtue, and without virtue there can be no liberty, and liberty is the object and life of all republican governments."

– Benjamin Rush, Essays, Literary, Moral and Philosophical (Philadelphia: Thomas and William Bradford, 1806), p. 8.)

Samuel Adams

Signer of the Declaration of Independence and Patriotic Leader

"A general dissolution of principles and manners will more surely overthrow the liberties of America than the whole force of the common enemy. While the people are virtuous they cannot be subdued; but when once they lose their virtue then will be ready to surrender their liberties to the first external or internal invader."

– A letter to James Warren dated February 12, 1779

Charles Carroll of Carrollton

Signer of the Declaration of Independence

"Without morals a republic cannot subsist any length of time; they therefore who are decrying the Christian religion, whose morality is so sublime & pure, [and] which denounces against the wicked eternal misery, and [which] insured to the good eternal happiness, are undermining the solid foundation of morals, the best security for the duration of free governments."

– Manuscript letter from Charles Carroll to Secretary of War, James McHenry, November 4, 1800.

John Quincy Adams

Sixth President of the United States

"There are three points of doctrine the belief of which forms the foundation of all morality. The first is the existence of God; the second is the immortality of the human soul; and the third is a future state of rewards and punishments. Suppose it possible for a man to disbelieve either of these three articles of faith and that man will have no conscience, he will have no other law than that of the tiger or the shark. The laws of man may bind him in chains or may put him to death, but they never can make him wise, virtuous, or happy."

– *John Quincy Adams, Letters of John Quincy Adams to His Son on the Bible and Its Teachings (Auburn: James M. Alden, 1850, pp. 22-23.)*

Bible Verses On Government

"Obey them that have the rule over you, and submit yourselves: for they watch for your souls, as they that must give account, that they may do it with joy, and not with grief: for that is unprofitable for you." *(Heb 13:17)*

"Submit yourselves to every ordinance of man for the Lord's sake: whether it be to the king, as supreme; Or unto governors, as unto them that are sent by him for the punishment of evildoers, and for the praise of them that do well. For so is the will of God, that with well doing ye may put to silence the ignorance of foolish men:As free, and not using your liberty for a cloke of maliciousness, but as the servants of God. Honour all men. Love the brotherhood. Fear God. Honour the king." *(1 Peter 2:13-17)*

[NOTE*: The United States is unique. Our government is established by the people for the good of the people. We give those in authority our consent and employ them to act on our behalf. The people also reserve rights and authority not given to the government. ("The powers not delegated to the United States by the Constitution, nor prohibited by it to the States, are reserved to the States respectively, or to the people." --10th Amendment of the Constitution) Therefore, in our republic, the people govern and are represented, not ruled.*]

"And Jesus answering said unto them, Render to Caesar the things that are Caesar's, and to God the things that are God's. And they marvelled at him." *(Mark 12:17)*

"If my people, which are called by my name, shall humble themselves, and pray, and seek my face, and turn from their wicked ways; then will I hear from heaven, and will forgive their sin, and will heal their land." *(2 Chronicles 7:14)*

"Be wise now therefore, O ye kings: be instructed, ye judges of the earth. Serve the LORD with fear, and rejoice with trembling. Kiss the Son, lest he be angry, and ye perish from the way, when his wrath is kindled but a little. Blessed are all they that put their trust in him." *(Psalm 2:10-12)*

"Give the king thy judgments, O God, and thy righteousness unto the king's son. He shall judge thy people with righteousness, and thy poor with judgment." *(Psalm 72:1-2)*

"I exhort therefore, that, first of all, supplications, prayers, intercessions, and giving of thanks, be made for all men; For kings, and for all that are in authority; that we may lead a quiet and peaceable life in all godliness and honesty. For this is good and acceptable in the sight of God our Saviour; Who will have all men to be saved, and to come unto the knowledge of the truth." *(1 Tim 2: 1-4)*

"When the righteous are in authority, the people rejoice: but when the wicked beareth rule, the people mourn." *(Proverbs 29:2)*

"It is an abomination to kings to commit wickedness: for the throne is established by righteousness." *(Proverbs 16:12)*

"The king that faithfully judgeth the poor, his throne shall be established for ever." *(Proverbs 29:14)*

"For the transgression of a land many are the princes thereof: but by a man of understanding and knowledge the state thereof shall be prolonged." *(Proverbs 28:2)*

"Put them in mind to be subject to principalities and powers, to obey magistrates, to be ready to every good work,To speak evil of no man, to be no brawlers, but gentle, shewing all meekness unto all men." *(Titus 3:1-2)*

"Then Peter and the other apostles answered and said, We ought to obey God rather than men." *(Acts 5:29)*

"Let every soul be subject unto the higher powers. For there is no power but of God: the powers that be are ordained of God. Whosoever therefore resisteth the power, resisteth the ordinance of God: and they that resist shall receive to themselves damnation. For rulers are not a terror to good works, but to the evil. Wilt thou then not be afraid of the power? do that which is good, and thou shalt have praise of the same: For he is the minister of God to thee for good. But if thou do that which is evil, be afraid; for he beareth not the sword in vain: for he is the minister of God, a revenger to execute wrath upon him that doeth evil. Wherefore ye must needs be subject, not only for wrath, but also for conscience sake. For for this cause pay ye tribute also: for they are God's ministers, attending continually upon this very thing. Render therefore to all their dues: tribute to whom tribute is due; custom to whom custom; fear to whom fear; honour to whom honour." *(Romans 13:1-7)*

[**NOTE***: Government should commend and promote what is right, moral, and beneficial for society. God established Government for justice and equal protection, not tyranny*]

Quotes From Historic Sermons of Clergy In Support of Liberty and Moral Government

Concerning Unlimited Submission and Non-Resistance to the Higher Powers

By: Rev. Jonathan Mayhew
(Preached January 30, 1750)

"The apostle enters upon his subject thus--Let every soul be subject unto the higher powers; for there is no power but of God: the powers that be, are ordained of God. Here he urges the duty of obedience from this topic of argument, that civil rulers, as they are supposed to fulfill the pleasure of God, are the ordinance of God. But how is this an argument for obedience to such rulers as do not perform the pleasure of God, by doing good; but the pleasure of the devil, by doing evil; and such as are not, therefore, God's ministers, but the devil's!

We may very safely assert these two things in general, without undermining government: **One is, That no civil rulers are to be obeyed when they enjoin things that are inconsistent with the commands of God**: All such disobedience is lawful and glorious; particularly, if persons refuse to comply with any legal establishment of religion, because it is a gross perversion and corruption (as to doctrine, worship and discipline) of a pure and divine religion, brought from heaven to earth by the Son of God, (the only King and Head of the Christian church) and propagated through the world by his inspired apostles. All commands running counter to the declared will of the supreme legislator of heaven and earth, are null and void: And therefore disobedience to them is a duty, not a crime."

The Christian Patriot

By: M. I. Motte
A Sermon Delivered at the South Congregational
Church, Boston,
(Preached July 5, 1840)

"If a majority of the citizens were sincere followers of
Jesus Christ, is it not evident, the councils of this
nation would be wiser and mightier, its progress more
glorious, its dominion even more potent than any the
world has ever seen? The day when it shall be resolved,
that the same evangelical principles shall govern states
that govern churches and gospel professors in their
private relations, would be the true jubilee of freedom.
That will be the mind's and the soul's declaration of
independence. That will be breaking every yoke at
length from body, and heart, and spirit. Thenceforth
slavery, in any form, would be but a tradition and a
name; whereas now it is the commonest of conditions,
and to the mass liberty is but a name; for he that
serveth any sin is the slave of sin. That day will come,
when the people choose. Choose it, resolve it, O my
brethren, as the first of civil duties. **Whatever your
party predilections, sacrifice them all for the
party of righteous men. Support no
administration, and oppose none, but on the
ground of moral principle.** Go with them as far as
Jesus Christ would go, and no further. Read the
constitution by the light of the Gospel. The Savior be
your paramount leader."

Proverbs 29:2

By: Isaac Beall, Pastor of the Baptist Church of Christ in Pawlet.

A Sermon Delivered Before His Excellency Jonas Galusha, Esq. Governor; His Honor Paul Brigham, Esq. Lieut. Governor, The Honorable Council, and The House of Representatives, of the State of Vermont, at Montpelier, on the Day of General Election,
(Preached Oct. 8, 1812)

"When the righteous are in authority, the people rejoice: but when the wicked beareth rule, the people mourn." *(Proverbs 29:2)*

"It being the great end of government to secure the civil happiness of the community, it is necessary and proper that the laws by which they consent to be governed should be as few, clear, and easy in their application as possible. For laws when needlessly multiplied become a vexatious and intolerable burden.

The laws of Jehovah being a transcript of perfect rectitude, there can be no reasonable objection raised against their being executed. In like manner, human laws ought to be as righteous and mild as to interest the community in their punctual execution, and in no instance fail of being enforced. It is necessary to civil happiness that government be supported and respected. But this will not be the case if good laws are evaded with impunity. What has a greater tendency to weaken the authority of a state than to continue laws in existence, which the powers that be cannot or care not to execute?

The scripture character of rulers is that they are not a terror to good works, but to the evil. Power is grossly abused and perverted when wicked citizens are fostered and protected by authority. God has ordained rulers to avenge the wrongs of injustice and oppression, and the violation of sedition and rebellion. No favor or friendship, no relation or connection with men in power, should secure the wicked from punishment. Righteous magistrates will, by the sword of justice, suppress immorality and every transgression of relative justice. **God commands it, and faithful subjects have a claim upon their rulers to be protected from fraud and oppression: to have the laws executed, their persons, their liberty, and their property protected from the depredations of lawless and unprincipled men."**

The Declaration of Independence:

A Transcription from the National Archives

IN CONGRESS, *July 4, 1776*.

The unanimous Declaration of the thirteen united States of America,

When in the Course of human events, it becomes necessary for one people to dissolve the political bands which have connected them with another, and to assume among the powers of the earth, the separate and equal station to which the Laws of Nature and of Nature's God entitle them, a decent respect to the opinions of mankind requires that they should declare the causes which impel them to the separation.

We hold these truths to be self-evident, that all men are created equal, that they are endowed by their Creator with certain unalienable Rights, that among these are Life, Liberty and the pursuit of Happiness.--That to secure these rights, **Governments are instituted among Men, deriving their just powers from the consent of the governed,** --That whenever any Form of Government becomes destructive of these ends, it is the Right of the People to alter or to abolish it, and to institute new Government, laying its foundation on such principles and organizing its powers in such form, as to them shall seem most likely to effect their Safety and Happiness. Prudence, indeed, will dictate that Governments long established should not be changed for light and transient causes; and accordingly all experience hath shewn, that mankind are more disposed to suffer, while evils are sufferable, than to right themselves by abolishing the forms to which they are accustomed. But when a long train of abuses and usurpations, pursuing invariably the same Object evinces a design to reduce them under absolute Despotism, it is their right, it is their duty, to throw off such Government, and to provide new Guards for their future security.--Such has been the patient sufferance of these Colonies; and such is now the necessity which constrains them to alter their former Systems of Government.

The history of the present King of Great Britain is a history of repeated injuries and usurpations, all having in direct object the establishment of an absolute Tyranny over these States. To prove this, let Facts be submitted to a candid world.

He has refused his Assent to Laws, the most wholesome and necessary for the public good.

– He has forbidden his Governors to pass Laws of immediate and pressing importance, unless suspended in their operation till his Assent should be obtained; and when so suspended, he has utterly neglected to attend to them.

– He has refused to pass other Laws for the accommodation of large districts of people, unless those people would relinquish the right of Representation in the Legislature, a right inestimable to them and formidable to tyrants only.

– He has called together legislative bodies at places unusual, uncomfortable, and distant from the depository of their public Records, for the sole purpose of fatiguing them into compliance with his measures.

– He has dissolved Representative Houses repeatedly, for opposing with manly firmness his invasions on the rights of the people.

– He has refused for a long time, after such dissolutions, to cause others to be elected; whereby the Legislative powers, incapable of Annihilation, have returned to the People at large for their exercise; the State remaining in the mean time exposed to all the dangers of invasion from without, and convulsions within.

– He has endeavoured to prevent the population of these States; for that purpose obstructing the Laws for Naturalization of Foreigners; refusing to pass others to encourage their migrations hither, and raising the conditions of new Appropriations of Lands.

– He has obstructed the Administration of Justice, by refusing his Assent to Laws for establishing Judiciary powers.

– He has made Judges dependent on his Will alone, for the tenure of their offices, and the amount and payment of their salaries.

– He has erected a multitude of New Offices, and sent hither swarms of Officers to harrass our people, and eat out their substance.

– He has kept among us, in times of peace, Standing Armies without the Consent of our legislatures.

– He has affected to render the Military independent of and superior to the Civil power.

– He has combined with others to subject us to a jurisdiction foreign to our constitution, and unacknowledged by our laws; giving his Assent to their Acts of pretended Legislation:

– For Quartering large bodies of armed troops among us:

– For protecting them, by a mock Trial, from punishment for any Murders which they should commit on the Inhabitants of these States:

– For cutting off our Trade with all parts of the world:

– For imposing Taxes on us without our Consent:

– For depriving us in many cases, of the benefits of Trial by Jury:

– For transporting us beyond Seas to be tried for pretended offences.

– For abolishing the free System of English Laws in a neighbouring Province, establishing therein an Arbitrary government, and enlarging its Boundaries so as to render it at once an example and fit instrument for introducing the same absolute rule into these Colonies:

– For taking away our Charters, abolishing our most valuable Laws, and altering fundamentally the Forms of our Governments:

– For suspending our own Legislatures, and declaring themselves invested with power to legislate for us in all cases whatsoever.

– He has abdicated Government here, by declaring us out of his Protection and waging War against us.

– He has plundered our seas, ravaged our Coasts, burnt our towns, and destroyed the lives of our people.

– He is at this time transporting large Armies of foreign Mercenaries to compleat the works of death, desolation and tyranny, already begun with circumstances of Cruelty & perfidy scarcely paralleled in the most barbarous ages, and totally unworthy the Head of a civilized nation.

– He has constrained our fellow Citizens taken Captive on the high Seas to bear Arms against their Country, to become the executioners of their friends and Brethren, or to fall themselves by their Hands.

– He has excited domestic insurrections amongst us, and has endeavoured to bring on the inhabitants of our frontiers, the merciless Indian Savages, whose known rule of warfare, is an undistinguished destruction of all ages, sexes and conditions.

In every stage of these Oppressions We have Petitioned for Redress in the most humble terms: Our repeated Petitions have been answered only by repeated injury. A Prince whose character is thus marked by every act which may define a Tyrant, is unfit to be the ruler of a free people. Nor have We been wanting in attentions to our Brittish brethren. We have warned them from time to time of attempts by their legislature to extend an unwarrantable jurisdiction over us. We have reminded them of the circumstances of our emigration and settlement here. We have appealed to their native justice and magnanimity, and we have conjured them by the ties of our common kindred to disavow these usurpations, which, would inevitably interrupt our connections and correspondence. They too have been deaf to the voice of justice and of consanguinity. We must, therefore, acquiesce in the necessity, which denounces our Separation, and hold them, as we hold the rest of mankind, Enemies in War, in Peace Friends.

We, therefore, the Representatives of the united States of America, in General Congress, Assembled, appealing to the Supreme Judge of the world for the rectitude of our intentions, do, in the Name, and by Authority of the good People of these Colonies, solemnly publish and declare, That these United Colonies are, and of Right ought to be Free and Independent States; that they are Absolved from all Allegiance to the British Crown, and that all political connection between them and the State of Great Britain, is and ought to be totally dissolved; and that as Free and Independent States, they have full Power to levy War, conclude Peace, contract Alliances, establish Commerce, and to do all other Acts and Things which Independent States may of right do.

And for the support of this Declaration, **with a firm reliance on the protection of divine Providence**, we mutually pledge to each other our Lives, our Fortunes and our sacred Honor.

The 56 signatures on the Declaration:

Georgia:
Button Gwinnett
Lyman Hall
George Walton

North Carolina:
William Hooper
Joseph Hewes
John Penn

South Carolina:
Edward Rutledge
Thomas Heyward, Jr.
Thomas Lynch, Jr.
Arthur Middleton

Maryland:
Samuel Chase
William Paca
Thomas Stone
Charles Carroll of Carrollton

Virginia:
George Wythe
Richard Henry Lee
Thomas Jefferson
Benjamin Harrison
Thomas Nelson, Jr.
Francis Lightfoot Lee
Carter Braxton

Pennsylvania:
Robert Morris
Benjamin Rush
Benjamin Franklin
John Morton
George Clymer
James Smith
George Taylor
James Wilson
George Ross

Delaware:
Caesar Rodney
George Read
Thomas McKean

New York:
William Floyd
Philip Livingston
Francis Lewis
Lewis Morris

New Jersey:
Richard Stockton
John Witherspoon
Francis Hopkinson
John Hart
Abraham Clark

New Hampshire:
Josiah Bartlett
William Whipple
Matthew Thornton

Massachusetts:
Samuel Adams
John Adams
Robert Treat Paine
Elbridge Gerry
John Hancock

Rhode Island:
Stephen Hopkins
William Ellery

Connecticut:
Roger Sherman
Samuel Huntington
William Williams
Oliver Wolcott

Picture: *Proposed Great Seal of The United States of America: "Rebellion to Tyrants is Obedience to God" by Benson Lossing, for Harper's New Monthly Magazine, July 1856.*

Proposed Seal for the United States

On July 4, 1776, Congress appointed Benjamin Franklin, Thomas Jefferson and John Adams "to bring in a device for a seal for the United States of America." Franklin's proposal adapted the biblical story of the parting of the Red Sea. Jefferson first recommended the "Children of Israel in the Wilderness, led by a Cloud by Day, and a Pillar of Fire by night. . . ." He then embraced Franklin's proposal and rewrote it.

Jefferson's revision of Franklin's proposal was presented by the committee to Congress on August 20. Although not accepted these drafts reveal the religious temper of the Revolutionary period. (source loc.gov)

The 50 State Constitutions

Acknowledge God and Religious Rights

The preamble, or content contained in each state constitution, shows reference to our creator who is the source of our rights. Information can be found on the official website of the state listed.

Alabama

"We the people of the State of Alabama, invoking the favor and guidance of Almighty God, do ordain and establish the following Constitution."

Alaska

"We the people of Alaska, grateful to God and to those who founded our nation and pioneered this great land, in order to secure and transmit to succeeding generations our heritage of political, civil, and religious liberty within the Union of States, do ordain and establish this constitution for the State of Alaska."

Arizona

"We the people of the State of Arizona, grateful to Almighty God for our liberties, do ordain this Constitution."

Arkansas

"We, the People of the State of Arkansas, grateful to
Almighty God for the privilege of choosing
our own form of government; for our civil and religious
liberty; and desiring to perpetuate its
blessings, and secure the same to our selves and
posterity; do ordain and establish this
Constitution."

California

"We, the People of the State of California, grateful to
Almighty God for our freedom, in order to secure and
perpetuate its blessings, do establish this Constitution."

Colorado

"We, the people of Colorado, with profound reverence
for the Supreme Ruler of the Universe, in order to form
a more independent and perfect government; establish
justice; insure tranquillity; provide for the common
defense; promote the general welfare and secure the
blessings of liberty to ourselves and our posterity, do
ordain and establish this constitution for the 'State of
Colorado'."

Connecticut

"The People of Connecticut acknowledging with
gratitude, the good providence of God, in having
permitted them to enjoy a free government; do, in
order more effectually to define, secure, and perpetuate
the liberties, rights and privileges which they have
derived from their ancestors; hereby, after a careful
consideration and revision, ordain and establish the
following constitution and form of civil government."

Delaware

"Through Divine goodness, all people have by nature the rights of worshiping and serving their Creator according to the dictates of their consciences, of enjoying and defending life and liberty, of acquiring and protecting reputation and property, and in general of obtaining objects suitable to their condition, without injury by one to another; and as these rights are essential to their welfare, for due exercise thereof, power is inherent in them; and therefore all just authority in the institutions of political society is derived from the people, and established with their consent, to advance their happiness; and they may for this end, as circumstances require, from time to time, alter their Constitution of government."

Florida

"We, the people of the State of Florida, being grateful to Almighty God for our constitutional liberty, in order to secure its benefits, perfect our government, insure domestic tranquility, maintain public order, and guarantee equal civil and political rights to all, do ordain and establish this constitution."

Georgia

"To perpetuate the principles of free government, insure justice to all, preserve peace, promote the interest and happiness of the citizen and of the family, and transmit to posterity the enjoyment of liberty, we the people of Georgia, relying upon the protection and guidance of Almighty God, do ordain and establish this Constitution."

Hawaii

We, the people of Hawaii, grateful for Divine Guidance, and mindful of our Hawaiian heritage and uniqueness as an island State, dedicate our efforts to fulfill the philosophy decreed by the Hawaii State motto, "Ua mau ke ea o ka aina i ka pono."

We reserve the right to control our destiny, to nurture the integrity of our people and culture, and to preserve the quality of life that we desire.

We reaffirm our belief in a government of the people, by the people and for the people, and with an understanding and compassionate heart toward all the peoples of the earth, do hereby ordain and establish this constitution for the State of Hawaii.

Idaho

"We, the people of the State of Idaho,grateful to Almighty God for our freedom,to secure its blessings and promote our common welfare do establish this Constitution."

Illinois

"We, the People of the State of Illinois - grateful to Almighty God for the civil, political and religious liberty which He has permitted us to enjoy and seeking His blessing upon our endeavors - in order to provide for the health, safety and welfare of the people; maintain a representative and orderly government; eliminate poverty and inequality; assure legal, social and economic justice; provide opportunity for the fullest development of the individual; insure domestic tranquility; provide for the common defense; and secure the blessings of freedom and liberty to ourselves and our posterity - do ordain and establish this Constitution for the State of Illinois."

Indiana

TO THE END, that justice be established, public order maintained, and liberty perpetuated; WE, the People of the State of Indiana, grateful to ALMIGHTY GOD for the free exercise of the right to choose our own form of government, do ordain this Constitution.

Iowa

"WE THE PEOPLE OF THE STATE OF IOWA, grateful to the Supreme Being for the blessings hitherto enjoyed, and feeling our dependence on Him for a continuation of those blessings, do ordain and establish a free and independent government, by the name of the State of Iowa..."

Kansas

"We, the people of Kansas, grateful to Almighty God for our civil and religious privileges, in order to insure the full enjoyment of our rights as American citizens, do ordain and establish this constitution of the state of Kansas..."

Kentucky

"We, the people of the Commonwealth of Kentucky, grateful to Almighty God for the civil, political and religious liberties we enjoy, and invoking the continuance of these blessings, do ordain and establish this Constitution."

Louisiana

"We, the people of Louisiana, grateful to Almighty God for the civil, political, economic, and religious liberties we enjoy, and desiring to protect individual rights to life, liberty, and property; afford opportunity for the fullest development of the individual; assure equality of rights; promote the health, safety, education, and welfare of the people; maintain a representative and orderly government; ensure domestic tranquility; provide for the common defense; and secure the blessings of freedom and justice to ourselves and our posterity, do ordain and establish this constitution."

Maine

"We the people of Maine, in order to establish justice, insure tranquility, provide for our mutual defense, promote our common welfare, and secure to ourselves and our posterity the blessings of liberty, acknowledging with grateful hearts the goodness of the Sovereign Ruler of the Universe in affording us an opportunity, so favorable to the design; and, imploring God's aid and direction in its accomplishment, do agree to form ourselves into a free and independent State, by the style and title of the State of Maine and do ordain and establish the following Constitution for the government of the same."

Maryland

"We, the People of the State of Maryland, grateful to Almighty God for our civil and religious liberty, and taking into our serious consideration the best means of establishing a good Constitution in this State for the sure foundation and more permanent security thereof, declare"

Massachusetts

"The end of the institution, maintenance, and administration of government, is to secure the existence of the body politic, to protect it, and to furnish the individuals who compose it with the power of enjoying in safety and tranquility their natural rights, and the blessings of life: and whenever these great objects are not obtained, the people have a right to alter the government, and to take measures necessary for their safety, prosperity and happiness.

The body politic is formed by a voluntary association of individuals: it is a social compact, by which the whole people covenants with each citizen, and each citizen with the whole people, that all shall be governed by certain laws for the common good. It is the duty of the people, therefore, in framing a constitution of government, to provide for an equitable mode of making laws, as well as for an impartial interpretation, and a faithful execution of them; that every man may, at all times, find his security in them.

We, therefore, the people of Massachusetts, acknowledging, with grateful hearts, the goodness of the great Legislator of the universe, in affording us, in the course of His providence, an opportunity, deliberately and peaceably, without fraud, violence or surprise, of entering into an original, explicit, and solemn compact with each other; and of forming a new constitution of civil government, for ourselves and posterity; and devoutly imploring His direction in so interesting a design, do agree upon, ordain and establish the following Declaration of Rights, and Frame of Government, as the Constitution of the Commonwealth of Massachusetts."

Michigan

"We, the people of the State of Michigan, grateful to Almighty God for the blessings of freedom, and earnestly desiring to secure these blessings undiminished to ourselves and our posterity, do ordain and establish this constitution."

Minnesota

"We, the people of the state of Minnesota, grateful to God for our civil and religious liberty, and desiring to perpetuate its blessings and secure the same to ourselves and our posterity, do ordain and establish this Constitution"

Mississippi

"We, the people of Mississippi in convention assembled, grateful to Almighty God, and invoking his blessing on our work, do ordain and establish this constitution."

Missouri

"We the people of Missouri, with profound reverence for the Supreme Ruler of the Universe, and grateful for His goodness, do establish this constitution for the better government of the state."

Montana

"We the people of Montana grateful to God for the quiet beauty of our state, the grandeur of our mountains, the vastness of our rolling plains, and desiring to improve the quality of life, equality of opportunity and to secure the blessings of liberty for this and future generations do ordain and establish this constitution."

Nebraska

"We, the people, grateful to Almighty God for our freedom, do ordain and establish the following declaration of rights and frame of government, as the Constitution of the State of Nebraska."

Nevada

"We the people of the State of Nevada Grateful to Almighty God for our freedom in order to secure its blessings, insure domestic tranquility, and form a more perfect Government, do establish this Constitution."

New Hampshire

"All men arc born equally free and independent; therefore, all government of right originates from the people, is founded in consent, and instituted for the general good. ...As morality and piety, rightly grounded on high principles, will give the best and greatest security to government, and will lay, in the hearts of men, the strongest obligations to due subjection; and as t he knowledge of these is most likely to be propagated through a society, therefore, the several parishes, bodies, corporate, or religious societies shall at all times have the right of electing their own teachers, and of contracting with them for their support or maintenance, or both. But no person shall ever be compelled to pay towards the support of the schools of any sect or denomination. And every person, denomination or sect shall be equally under the protection of the law; and no subordination of any one sect, denomination or persuasion to another shall ever be established." (Article 1 and 6 of the New Hampshire Constitution)

New Jersey

"We, the people of the State of New Jersey, grateful to Almighty God for the civil and religious liberty which He hath so long permitted us to enjoy, and looking to Him for a blessing upon our endeavors to secure and transmit the same unimpaired to succeeding generations, do ordain and establish this Constitution."

New Mexico

"We, the people of New Mexico, grateful to Almighty God for the blessings of liberty, in order to secure the advantages of a state government, do ordain and establish this constitution."

New York

"We The People of the State of New York, grateful to Almighty God for our Freedom, in order to secure its blessings, DO ESTABLISH THIS CONSTITUTION."

North Carolina

"We, the people of the State of North Carolina, grateful to Almighty God, the Sovereign Ruler of Nations, for the preservation of the American Union and the existence of our civil, political and religious liberties, and acknowledging our dependence upon Him for the continuance of those blessings to us and our posterity, do, for the more certain security thereof and for the better government of this State, ordain and establish this Constitution."

North Dakota

"We, the people of North Dakota, grateful to Almighty God for the blessings of civil and

religious liberty, do ordain and establish this constitution."

Ohio

"We, the people of the State of Ohio, grateful to Almighty God for our freedom, to secure its blessings and promote our common welfare, do establish this Constitution."

Oklahoma

"Invoking the guidance of Almighty God, in order to secure and perpetuate the blessing of liberty; to secure just and rightful government; to promote our mutual welfare and happiness, we, the people of the State of Oklahoma, do ordain and establish this Constitution."

Oregon

"We the people of the State of Oregon to the end that Justice be established, order maintained, and liberty perpetuated, do ordain this Constitution ...We declare that all men, when they form a social compact are equal in right: that all power is inherent in the people, and all free governments are founded on their authority, and instituted for their peace, safety, and happiness; and they have at all times a right to alter, reform, or abolish the government in such manner as they may think proper.– ...All men shall be secure in the Natural right, to worship Almighty God according to the dictates of their own consciences." (Preamble; and Article 1, sections 1 and 2.)

Pennsylvania

"WE, the people of the Commonwealth of Pennsylvania, grateful to Almighty God for the blessings of civil and religious liberty, and humbly invoking His guidance, do ordain and establish this Constitution."

Rhode Island

"We, the people of the State of Rhode Island and Providence Plantations, grateful to Almighty God for the civil and religious liberty which He hath so long permitted us to enjoy, and looking to Him for a blessing upon our endeavors to secure and to transmit the same, unimpaired, to succeeding generations, do ordain and establish this Constitution of government."
South Carolina
"We, the people of the State of South Carolina, in Convention assembled, grateful to God for our liberties, do ordain and establish this Constitution for the preservation and perpetuation of the same."

South Dakota

"We, the people of South Dakota, grateful to Almighty God for our civil and religious liberties, in order to form a more perfect and independent government, establish justice, insure tranquillity, provide for the common defense, promote the general welfare and preserve to ourselves and to our posterity the blessings of liberty, do ordain and establish this Constitution for the state of South Dakota."

Tennessee

"Whereas, The people of the territory of the United States south of the river Ohio, having the right of admission into the general government as a member state thereof, consistent with the Constitution of the United States, and the act of cession of the state of North Carolina, recognizing the ordinance for the government of the territory—of the United States north west of the Ohio River, by their delegates and representatives in convention assembled, did on the sixth day of February, in the year of our Lord one thousand seven hundred and ninetysix,
ordain and establish a Constitution, or form of government, and mutually agreed with each other to form themselves into a free and independent state by the name of the state of Tennessee"

Texas

"Humbly invoking the blessings of Almighty God, the people of the State of Texas, do ordain and establish this Constitution."

Utah

"Grateful to Almighty God for life and liberty, we, the people of Utah, in order to secure and perpetuate the principles of free government, do ordain and establish this CONSTITUTION."

Vermont

"That all persons are born equally free and independent, and have certain natural, inherent, and unalienable rights, amongst which are the enjoying and defending life and liberty, acquiring, possessing and protecting property, and pursuing and obtaining happiness and safety; therefore no person born in this country, or brought from over sea, ought to be holden by law, to serve any person as a servant, slave or apprentice, after arriving to the age of twenty-one years, unless bound by the person's own consent, after arriving to such age, or bound by law for the payment of debts, damages, fines, costs, or the like...That all persons have a natural and unalienable right, to worship Almighty God, according to the dictates of their own consciences and understandings, as in their opinion shall be regulated by the word of God; and that no person ought to, or of right can be compelled to attend any religious worship, or erect or support any place of worship, or maintain any minister, contrary to the dictates of conscience, nor can any person be justly deprived or abridged of any civil right as a citizen, on account of religious sentiments, or peculia[r] mode of religious worship; and that no authority can, or ought to be vested in, or assumed by, any power whatever, that shall in any case interfere with, or in any manner control the rights of conscience, in the free exercise of religious worship. Nevertheless, every sect or denomination of Christians ought to observe the sabbath or Lord's day, and keep up some sort of religious worship, which to them shall seem most agreeable to the revealed will of God." (Articles 1 and 3)

Virginia

"A DECLARATION OF RIGHTS made by the good people of Virginia in the exercise of their sovereign powers, which rights do pertain to them and their posterity, as the basis and foundation of government... That all men are by nature equally free and independent and have certain inherent rights, of which, when they enter into a state of society, they cannot, by any compact, deprive or divest their posterity; namely, the enjoyment of life and liberty, with the means of acquiring and possessing property, and pursuing and obtaining happiness and safety...That all power is vested in, and consequently derived from, the people, that magistrates are their trustees and servants, and at all times amenable to them...That religion or the duty which we owe to our Creator, and the manner of discharging it, can be directed only by reason and conviction, not by force or violence; and, therefore, all men are equally entitled to the free exercise of religion, according to the dictates of conscience; and that it is the mutual duty of all to practice Christian forbearance, love, and charity towards each other. No man shall be compelled to frequent or support any religious worship, place, or ministry whatsoever, nor shall be enforced, restrained, molested, or burthened in his body or goods, nor shall otherwise suffer on account of his religious opinions or belief; but all men shall be free to profess and by argument to maintain their opinions in matters of religion, and the same shall in nowise diminish, enlarge, or affect their civil capacities. And the General Assembly shall not prescribe any religious test whatever, or confer any peculiar privileges or advantages on any sect or denomination, or pass any law requiring or authorizing any religious society, or the people of any district within this Commonwealth, to levy on themselves or others, any tax for the erection or repair of any house of public worship, or for the support of any church or ministry; but it shall be left free to every person to select his religious instructor, and to make for his support such private contract as he shall please." (Article 1, Bill of Rights; sections 1, 2, and 16)

Washington

"We, the people of the State of Washington, grateful to the Supreme Ruler of the Universe for our liberties, do ordain this constitution."

West Virginia

"Since through Divine Providence we enjoy the blessings of civil, political and religious liberty, we, the people of West Virginia, in and through the provisions of this Constitution, reaffirm our faith in and constant reliance upon God and seek diligently to promote, preserve and perpetuate good government in the state of West Virginia for the common welfare, freedom and security of ourselves and our posterity."

Wisconsin

"We, the people of Wisconsin, grateful to Almighty God for our freedom, in order to secure its blessings, form a more perfect government, insure domestic tranquility and promote the general welfare, do establish this constitution."

Wyoming

"We, the people of the State of Wyoming, grateful to God for our civil, political and religious liberties, and desiring to secure them to ourselves and perpetuate them to our posterity, do ordain and establish this Constitution."